BOLD KIDS

MW01674927

Buddhism

AMAZING AND INTRIGUING FACTS
CHILDREN'S RELIGION BOOK

Learn about Buddhism's beliefs and practice in this book! Buddhists follow a vow to live in peace and meditate in monasteries. They do not believe in God or the soul. They do not worship animals or other living things.

And, of course, you'll want to know about their beliefs and practices! Keep reading to learn all the fascinating facts about Buddhism! And, don't forget to check out our book on Buddhist symbols! You'll be amazed at all the fascinating facts about Buddhism!

BUDDHISTS BELIEVE IN PEACE

Buddhist doctrine has long been associated with peace and harmony. It has been a source of morality and justice for rulers and societies alike, and a means to personal salvation. Yet as Buddhism has evolved over the centuries, it has also suffered changes of its own.

Early sixth century Chinese monks launched revolts to defend their religion. Today, Buddhist monks in Thailand and Burma continue to fight violently for their faith. These conflicts, like the rest of Buddhism's cycle of violence, are indicative of a declining Buddhist religion.

As Buddhists, we can't ignore the importance of peace. Buddha taught us to live in harmony with nature and to cultivate a balanced life. He emphasized the importance of regulating impulses and behaviors to promote peace.

Buddha also stressed self-awareness and reflection. Buddhism promotes inner reflection and the development of compassionate actions. Buddhism believes that the root of violence lies in the mind, and that peace can be achieved only when the mind is calm and focused.

Buddhists are concerned about the motives behind killings. In Sri Lanka, Buddhist monks chant with soldiers to bless them after they kill someone. This shows that they oppose violence, preferring to keep soldiers cool in the face of danger.

The Tibetan Dalai Lama also spoke of the importance of "intention" when asked about the self-immolations in Tibet. It is important to remember that there are people in every religion, and Buddhism is no different.

A Buddhist vision of the world is a place where all life is sacred, in which selfishness is not interfered with, and where everyone has the potential to attain enlightenment. By taking these three steps, we can live in peace.

These three steps are simple and practical, but they're important, as they lead to a more peaceful world. But how can we achieve peace? Let's look at them in more detail.

Buddhism teaches that all life is interdependent and not qualitatively different from human life. For example, Buddhist teachings claim that when an animal dies, it experiences resentment, hatred, and revenge, which poisons the animal's flesh.

And, when humans kill animals, these thoughts are broadcast to both the killer and the victim. Therefore, Buddhism views human life as an equal. This is an important part of Buddhism's history, and we should respect it.

THEY DO NOT BELIEVE IN GOD OR THE SOUL

The polar opposites of Buddhism and Hinduism, both of which believe in the existence of a "soul," are irreconcilable. Both reject the idea of post-mortem existence, and both make one fundamental mistake.

Buddhism denies the existence of the soul, but not in the same way as Hinduism. Hinduism does believe in reincarnation, but Buddhists don't believe in rebirth.

The Middle-Way of Buddhism is sometimes called the Middle Path. This term describes the middle way between hedonism and asceticism. The Buddha often referred to his path as the middle way.

Many Buddhists refer to the doctrine of dependent origination as the "middle way" between these two extremes. It is difficult to define the relationship between the two philosophies. However, Buddhists disagree with each other on the relationship between God and the soul.

The four basic categories of reality in the Abhidhamma are Rupa (the body), Citta (mental matter), Cetasika (unconditioned) and Nibbana, or "soul."

The Buddha is the most important source of value, and therefore, the ideal is the ultimate goal. The Buddha's life has meaning and importance for the human race, which explains why he was called Buddha.

Buddha lived a simple life until he found insight. Later, he developed great wisdom and became a great teacher, whose compassion enabled him to help others awaken. Historically, the idea of a god has been a source of endless debate throughout the world.

The Buddha argued that belief in an eternal God obstructed the path to enlightenment. However, this idea is not universal and Buddhism teaches that it is essential to find the truth of our existence.

The Buddha also rejected the idea of a soul. Buddhism also denies the existence of a humanlike god. However, Buddhists do acknowledge the existence of devas and bodhisattvas. The Buddha himself was a human, but never claimed to be a god.

Instead, he led a saintly life and taught others how to achieve nirvana. Consequently, Buddhists believe that the Buddha's teachings were based on a rational, logical, and humanistic approach to life.

THEY CELEBRATE EVERY QUARTER OF THE MOON

In Buddhism, every quarter of the lunar calendar is a special day, and Buddhists celebrate it with festivals and ceremonies. The full moon in June and July is called Waso and is celebrated with free food and rituals.

The disciples offer robes to the monks during a ceremony called Waso Robe-Offering. The full moon on Waso is significant in Buddhism because it is the date of the Buddha's birth, first sermon, and miracles.

The 15th day of the seventh lunar month is Ghost Festival. It is said that on this day, the gates to Hell open and the souls of the dead visit loved ones to thank them for teaching them abhidhamma.

The hungry spirits are fed with food on this day, which is believed to bring them good luck in the coming year. Buddhists also make offerings to the dead on this day, as well as to their living parents.

Buddhists also observe the full moon of the month of Thadingyut. This festival falls around the end of the Buddhist Lent. During the festival, lanterns are lit at pagodas and houses to honor the Buddha and his teachings.

The Mahamuni temple also celebrates a lighting festival, which occurs at the end of the Buddhist Lent. A candle procession is also held during the full moon.

The full moon day of the eighth lunar month is the Asalha Puja, commemorating the Buddha's first sermon to the first ascetics. It also commemorates the day Kondanna attained the level of mind purity known as Sotapanna.

This ceremony marks the end of the Rains retreat and is followed by the Kathina ceremony where the laity make formal offerings to the Sangha.

CPSIA information can be obtained
at www.ICGtesting.com
Printed in the USA
LVHW071604161222
735372LV00007B/252

9 781071 718360